"There's the old freedom song that goes, 'Until the killing of black men is as important as the killing of white men, we who believe in freedom cannot rest.' This book is a powerful freedom song from two veterans of the movement. It is a reminder that until black lives matter, the idea that all lives matter is still just an aspiration."

Shane Claiborne, author; activist

"This is an important book written by men who have given their entire lives to the ministry of reconciliation. I read it straight through and was both challenged and inspired! You will be too."

Bill Hybels, senior pastor, Willow Creek Community Church; founder, Global Leadership Summit

"Wayne Gordon and John Perkins have given their lives to racial reconciliation and to working out the implications of the gospel for community life in the city of God. Here they speak a prophetic word about America's racial strife—past and present—and offer a hopeful vision for a future where black lives (and all lives) matter. As close friends in Christian leadership, these two friends have written a book that is especially important for white evangelicals to read and discuss."

Philip Ryken, president, Wheaton College

"An excellent book at a critical time. Candid, compassionate, confrontational. It offers a practical path toward greater mutual understanding and reconciliation in a nation whose racial wounds have once again been laid bare."

Bob Lupton, founder, FCS Urban Ministries Atlanta; author, *Toxic Charity*

"*Do All Lives Matter?* addresses the most pressing issue of our day: Do black lives, and the lives of people of color, matter in our society? Instead of offering easy answers, John and Coach provide us with biblical and practical insights they have been living out for decades that challenge us to reject hate and work to dismantle racism in our neighborhoods and in our nation. Timely and powerful."

Noel Castellanos, president, Christian Community Development Association

"There has never been a moment in US history when our nation has proclaimed that 'all lives *do not* matter.' John Perkins and Wayne Gordon, two of the most significant leaders in the evangelical movement and quest for biblical compassion and justice, present a cogent and passionate argument that throughout US history, and within our current social reality, our nation has repeatedly asserted that 'black lives *do not* matter.' This timely book reminds twenty-first-century US Christians of the need to proclaim a prophetic truth in the midst of troubled times. For the sake of the name of our Savior, please read and receive the key message of this important work."

Soong-Chan Rah, professor of church growth and evangelism, North Park Theological Seminary; author, *Prophetic Lament* and *Return to Justice*

"Open this book to read about courage; about biblical conviction; about steely determination; about a refusal to back down; about pain, grief, and tears; and keep reading because in this book you will eventually see that Wayne Gordon and John Perkins know that today's pain can be redeemed by kingdom hope."

Scot McKnight, Julius R. Mantey Professor of New Testament, Northern Seminary

"Dealing with a topic that all too often has been called forth because of violence, Coach Wayne Gordon and Dr. John Perkins have given us a book of hope. That is not to say that it glosses over the injustices and fears that are a part of our society. Far from it. But the book provides compelling stories that will deepen our understanding across the racial divides that have been and still are in our country—if we will listen to the stories well. It has practical helps that, empowered by the work of the God who loves to heal broken things in his world, could bring us closer together as a people. Dr. Perkins and Coach Gordon have lived lives committed to reconciliation. Together they have given us a book that could help us live in a way that declares all lives truly matter in a world in which some lives, particularly those embodied by people of color, don't seem to matter. I recommend it highly to you."

Greg Waybright, senior pastor, Lake Avenue Church

"I must admit that words cannot express and thoughts cannot bring to one's imagination how relevant this book is for such a time as this. In this work John and Wayne have challenged us both individually and as a nation to truly understand that we have a date with destiny. This destiny has arrived, and we must ask ourselves, 'Are we willing to be teachable and humble enough to learn from one another and appreciate each other's journey?' This book echoes the words of Dr. Martin Luther King Jr., 'We must come together as brothers or we will perish as fools.'"

Carey Casey, ambassador for fathers, National Center for Fathering

"This book helps us understand why 'Black Lives Matter' really means all lives matter. The lives that have mattered least in human society will be the lives that must matter most in pursuit of justice and the kingdom of God. John and Coach share the difficult things we must talk about before we can talk about true reconciliation."

Marshall Hatch, senior pastor, New Mount Pilgrim Missionary Baptist Church, Chicago

"*All* lives matter, but when some come to believe they matter less, that they're invisible or a problem, God's people need to talk—and even more, to listen. John Perkins and Wayne Gordon speak from the heart, and my heart needs to listen, and learn, and act. Personal, practical, passionate, faithful! I urge my fellow followers of Christ to read this and go beyond reading, to reach beyond comfort, so race might not be allowed the last word."

John Crosby, senior pastor, Christ Presbyterian
Church, Edina, Minnesota

"Three score and seven years ago my parents brought forth in Evanston a new baby, conceived in Manhasset and dedicated to the proposition that all babies are important. Now we have a wonderful book, *Do All Lives Matter?* by Wayne Gordon and John Perkins. It is altogether fitting and proper that we should read this."

Pat McCaskey, vice president, Chicago Bears

"This book is a great tool in our struggle to stop prejudice, racism, and senseless violence in our country. Reading this will help us get on the journey of reconciliation and building the Beloved Community where we treat each other with the respect and reverence that demonstrate that all our lives matter."

Rev. Michael L. Pfleger, pastor, Faith Community of St. Sabina

"Such a good word for so crucial a time in the church and in our nation! Bravo, Coach and JP! The principles of this book have been forged in the crucible of your lives for decades and give us hope to press on despite the challenges. God give us those tears of compassion, heartfelt prayer, and practical neighbor-love that you call us to. May *all* lives matter to us as they do to him!"

John Fuder, Heart for the City, PRAYChicago

"John Perkins and Coach Gordon change the conversation about police and racism. They challenge the body of Christ to step away from #hashtags and walk in the shoes of another person. Drawing from their experiences today, they offer constructive, biblical solutions for any church to apply to their city. They show us how to confront racism, reconcile people to Jesus, and offer hope to communities."

William D. Shiell, president and professor of pastoral
theology and preaching,
Northern Seminary

"In a time of intense racial polarization, two of evangelicalism's most trusted voices on reconciliation bring us back to the basics: a biblically based, gospel-centered call to love God and neighbor, especially in the face of injustice. This is the place to begin for those exploring why Christian faithfulness demands affirming the value of black lives."

Greg Lee, assistant professor of theology, Wheaton College

"As the pastor of a predominantly white church, I have struggled with my congregation to make sense of the agony of our racially charged times. In this remarkable book, Drs. Gordon and Perkins have given me the resource I wish I had in my hands all along. This is a brilliantly balanced, biblical, and eye-opening treatment of a subject that must matter more to all of us who love God and our nation, no matter what our skin color or politics. Moreover, this book provides practical action steps that churches and individuals can take to begin to shape a better America."

Daniel Meyer, senior pastor, Christ Church of Oak Brook

"In *Do All Lives Matter?*, I'm encouraged by the courageous effort of Dr. Wayne Gordon and Dr. John Perkins to offer a probing and prophetic critique of race relations in American society in the new millennium. Moreover, as Drs. Gordon and Perkins share from passionate hearts and their own uniquely personal narratives on race, I'm reminded of Ralph Ellison's seminal work *The Invisible Man*. In a day when many misinformed Americans believe we live in a post-racial society, I celebrate *Do All Lives Matter?* for shining the light of prophetic truth so that the many marginalized Americans suffering from what Ellison calls 'invisibility' might enjoy the liberating power of truth revealed."

Vance Henry, deputy chief of staff, Mayor Rahm Emanuel

"Coach and John Perkins have been not just working in the community but living in the heart of the community for over four decades now. Their commitment, leadership, and courage are extraordinary. As much as their daily work inspires all of us who strive to make a difference, so too does their writing—we owe it to ourselves to listen and learn."

Arne Duncan, former US Secretary of Education

"For too long the church has been in denial about our implicit and explicit contributions to the construction of a sinful and unjust hierarchy of lives that prioritizes white-ness and male-ness. Coach and John Perkins make a case for why Christians must acknowledge that although 'All Lives Matter' is an honorable aspiration drawn from an image-of-God theology, it is not our current reality. They invite Christians who are sincere in their pursuit of Jesus and the biblical love of neighbor to imagine and join in the sacrificial work toward creating a just kingdom society where all lives do matter."

Mayra Macedo-Nolan, board chairwoman, Christian Community Development Association; associate pastor of community outreach, Lake Avenue Church

DO ALL LIVES
MATTER?

DO ALL LIVES MATTER?

The Issues We Can No Longer Ignore
and the Solutions We All Long For

WAYNE GORDON
and JOHN M. PERKINS

BakerBooks

a division of Baker Publishing Group
Grand Rapids, Michigan

Published by Baker Books
a division of Baker Publishing Group
P.O. Box 6287, Grand Rapids, MI 49516-6287
www.bakerbooks.com

Printed in the United States of America

Library of Congress Cataloging-in-Publication Data
Names: Gordon, Wayne, author.
Title: Do all lives matter? / Wayne Gordon and John M. Perkins.
Description: Grand Rapids : Baker Books, 2017. | Includes bibliographical references and index.
Identifiers: LCCN 2016045576 | ISBN 9780801075339 (pbk. : alk. paper)
Subjects: LCSH: United States—Race relations. | Race relations—Religious aspects—Christianity. | Racism—United States. | Racism—Religious aspects—Christianity. | Reconciliation—Religious aspects—Christianity.| Black lives matter movement.
Classification: LCC E185.615.G667 2017 | DDC 305.800973—dc23
LC record available at https://lccn.loc.gov/2016045576

We dedicate this book to all the people
who have felt that their lives did not matter.
Our hope is that they will experience God's great love
for them and will know that their lives do matter.

Contents

Foreword

Another heartbreaking headline: "A Grim Milestone: Chicago Surpasses 2015 Homicide Toll."* By September 5, 2016, there had been over five hundred deaths—and counting.

Every morning paper, every evening news, brings us more reports of gun violence and death in Chicago. Videos showing unwarranted police violence. Stories of first-grade boys lured into alleys and executed in gang retaliation. Pregnant mothers shot. Grandmothers gunned down holding toddlers' hands. After hundreds of such tragic stories, emotions start to shut down.

But for "Coach" Wayne Gordon, these are not numbers and random stories. These are his neighbors in Lawndale. These are his friends at his church. This battle against racism, poverty, and violence is his life.

More than forty years ago, Wayne Gordon and his wife, Anne, decided to live their faith and make their home in Lawndale, one of the most dangerous sections of Chicago. It was not an easy decision for this white couple to make their stand on those mean

*"A Grim Milestone: Chicago Surpasses 2015 Homicide Toll," *Chicago Tribune*, September 5, 2016, http://www.chicagotribune.com/news/media/ct-a-grim-mile stone-chicago-surpasses-2015-homicide-toll-video-20160906-premiumvideo.html.

streets. But the Lawndale Community Church they started is now a positive force for change: renovating apartments, building a first-class fitness center, mentoring students, running a medical clinic, leading an effort to bring restorative justice to the neighborhood, and clinging to a Lou Malnati's Pizza Restaurant to prove this part of Chicago can sustain a mainstream business.

When you read this book, which Coach Gordon wrote with his longtime friend John Perkins, you can feel the pain and the promise in their words. Troubled, angered, challenged by the "Black Lives Matter"/"All Lives Matter" debate, they wrote this book to chart a path that looks honestly at our nation's battle with racism. Their take on the "invisible people" in America and the common ground we must find is inspired by their faith.

When Coach Gordon struggled with the divisive national debate and the endless deaths, he found his footing by visiting the churches of his fellow ministers and praying with his neighbors and church family, and in the wisdom of his eighty-six-year-old "best friend," John Perkins.

Wayne Gordon is clearly not lost in prayer. He is led by prayer. In chapter 8 he challenges us to change our hearts and practice what we preach. His suggestions of specific actions we can take to demonstrate that all lives matter is the heart of this short and powerful book.

Where many have lost hope, these two men have not.

As Coach Gordon writes: "Always live believing that what is good and right and true and just will, in God's time, emerge victorious. All lives do matter!"

US Senator Dick Durbin

Introduction

A Sense of Urgency

I (Wayne) awoke on Sunday morning, July 10, 2016, with the deep conviction that something had to be done. Few would challenge the contention that violence in our country—including violence surrounding issues of race—has reached epidemic proportions. Police shootings of African American men and turmoil in our streets—including in the predominantly African American community of North Lawndale in Chicago, which I've called home for more than four decades—are so common it's becoming hard to consider them news.

The violence, of course, is not confined to issues of race. No doubt, many of the nearly 350 murders in Chicago recorded in the first half of 2016 alone had nothing to do with race. Nor are the killings limited to confrontations among individuals. Along with millions of Americans and others around the world, I experience some mixture of grief, fear, anger, confusion, and helplessness each time the TV screens and headlines are dominated by news of yet another mass killing—whether purposefully evil or completely senseless.

Over the years, in sermons to my congregation and in individual counseling sessions, I have from time to time encouraged people to resist feeling overly burdened by the problems of the world. After all, it's easy to feel completely powerless when contemplating the magnitude of the challenges we face. Knowing that we can't do *everything*, we can fall victim to a kind of emotional and spiritual paralysis that prevents us from doing *anything*.

Of course I know I can't solve the world's problems. But I awoke on July 10 with a profound sense of urgency and determination to do *something*—to exercise whatever influence I might have to push back against the violence, the hatred, the intolerance, and the insensitivity that results in some people feeling insignificant, inferior, and unequal—in short, feeling that their lives don't matter.

I talked with my wife, Anne, who immediately supported the idea that something had to be done. Anne and I have been moved to tears many more times than we can count. Our hearts are often heavy and our spirits often burdened from more than forty years of shootings and other tragedies in Lawndale. This includes the tragedy of people we love being treated in ways that communicate—in subtle and sometimes not-so-subtle ways—that their lives don't matter.

On the morning of July 10, I also called John Perkins to share with him the sense of urgency and conviction I was feeling. Now eighty-six years old, John has been my mentor for more than thirty-five years. At some point along the way he also became my best friend. As an African American, John has many times throughout his life—especially as a child and young man—been on the receiving end of messages that communicated his life doesn't matter. I asked him if he would be willing to share his story and perspectives for this book, and he immediately agreed, proffering, "Let's do it now. Let's do it fast. We've got to do something to right the direction we've been heading in."

This short book is our attempt to do just that: to help change the direction in which we are headed. And to do so as quickly as possible. For our current state of affairs pits law enforcement against the public and individuals against each other. And inasmuch as things seem to be getting worse instead of better, we cannot procrastinate any longer. The time for justice is now. The time for proclaiming and living the truth that *all* lives matter is now. The time for building a culture of peace and respect to replace a culture of violence and hatred is now. In short, now is the time for becoming the "beloved community."

Anne and I have experienced a taste of what I believe Dr. King had in mind when he spoke or wrote about the beloved community.* We have found our North Lawndale community on the city's West Side to be a place dominated by love and kindness. People have cared for us in ways too numerous to detail here. They have come to our rescue in the middle of crises.

In a country where so many suburbanites enter their homes through garages and thus don't even know their next door neighbors' names, we know and love all of those who live nearby. Mr. Carson, the Lewises, the Littles, the Townsells, the Worthys, Willie, James, Michael, Tony, and Jerry could not be more loving or kind neighbors. In all we do, they look out for us and we for them. Especially when I am away from home, our neighbors watch out for Anne, making sure she is doing well and is safe. At Lawndale Community Church, every other week we stand so people can share their prayer requests and praises. This is one of the many ways in which we feel knitted together as a church family and a community.

Yet we know that danger lurks not far away. In fact, I consider it the height of irony that in the midst of the poverty, chaos, and violence of a stereotypically tough urban area, we experience daily the blessings of a warm, caring, beloved community.

---

*For more information, see "The King Philosophy: The Beloved Community," The King Center, accessed September 16, 2016, http://www.thekingcenter.org/king-philosophy.

These are blessings John and I long for others to know and experience. And it begins with the genuine understanding that all lives truly do matter. It is our hope that this book will help to build this understanding, in part by recognizing and fully appreciating why some people have come to feel their lives don't matter.

We acknowledge up front that our purpose is not to provide an in-depth study of the issues we introduce. Some will no doubt be frustrated by the lack of analysis of issues or events we mention in the book. To the extent this happens, we suggest making it part of your discussions and interactions with others, including those whose perspectives might differ from your own.

Our purpose is simply to get people talking and coming together with an openness to new understandings and perspectives. We want to be part of the process of healing the racial and cultural divides that have led to so much violence and pain. And we pursue this goal by exploring the ramifications of the affirmation, "All lives matter."

1

A Movement Is Born

Do all lives matter? On the surface, the answer seems obvious. Of course all lives matter! This conviction lies at the core of America's identity and has since our nation's beginning. The Declaration of Independence states, "We hold these truths to be self-evident, that all men are created equal, that they are endowed by their Creator with certain unalienable Rights."

The affirmation that all lives matter is consistent also with Christian faith and core theology. All human beings are created in the image of God, and the Scriptures could not be more clear that all are equal in God's eyes.

What we must recognize, however, is that the concept of all people being equal—and all lives mattering equally—exists as an aspiration, not as a reality. To put it another way: it exists in theory but has never existed in practice. After all, many of the men who signed the Declaration of Independence owned slaves. And the document they signed specified equal rights only for one gender. We can either call the Declaration's signers hypocrites or credit them for holding up an ideal for the nation to pursue.

Of course, much has changed in the nearly two and a half centuries since that Declaration was signed. Slavery ended more than 150 years ago. Today, women not only can vote but can hold any political office. Yet if we are to be honest, we must acknowledge that in 2016 people are still routinely treated unequally—both legally and socially—based on factors ranging from how much money they make to social status and family pedigree to ethnicity and skin color to physical ability or disability to height and weight and how good-looking they are. Does anyone really think that television weatherpersons got the job based on how well they did in their college meteorology courses?

Determining how fair things are for individuals or groups can be complicated. After all, it's possible for the same people to be discriminated against in some settings while being favored in others. For example, it's well documented that an African American male is more likely to be treated unfairly by our justice system than a Caucasian person. But when applying for a job, that same African American male might get preferential treatment from an employer committed to hiring minorities, even if he grew up with more social and financial advantages than his white counterpart.

Because there are so many angles from which to analyze particular cases of alleged injustice—and different criteria for determining what is fair and right—it can be challenging to reach definitive conclusions. But the complexity should not prevent us from recognizing trends and realities that are difficult, if not impossible, to deny. It should not, for example, stop us from asking why—more than 150 years after the demise of slavery and several decades removed from the Civil Rights revolution—so many African American people in our country feel the need for the movement "Black Lives Matter."

Consider that many African American people would testify that there has never been a time when they haven't been mistreated by law enforcement. Modern technology, including cell phone videos, has only brought the issue more squarely into the public eye.

The highly publicized 2012 killing of Trayvon Martin in San-ford, Florida, was a turning point, one that gave birth to the term "Black Lives Matter" and to organized protests calling for justice. A vigilante named George Zimmerman shot and killed Martin, a teenage boy, while he was walking home from a store. Of course we know how this story ended. Zimmerman's acquittal spawned outcries from African American communities across the country.

In July 2014, forty-three-year-old Eric Garner was stopped by New York City police for selling loose cigarettes. He was wrestled to the ground as a police officer put his head in a chokehold. The incident was captured on video. Garner can be heard saying "I can't breathe" eleven times. The New York medical examiner officially ruled this case a homicide. But in December 2014, a grand jury decided not to indict the officer, sending the message to African Americans across this land that their lives do not matter.

After Michael Brown was shot and killed by a white police of-ficer in Ferguson, Missouri, on August 9, 2014, "Black Lives Mat-ter" evolved from slogan to movement. Brown, though unarmed, was killed by Darren Wilson apparently for stealing a few dollars' worth of merchandise. The movement added the slogan, "Hands up, don't shoot."

There are many more cases, but these three alone establish that being black in America can be difficult and dangerous. Each of these three persons received a death sentence for walking home, selling cigarettes, or minor theft. The effect of their experiences has gone far beyond their grieving families. It has sounded a chord that resonates deep in the lives of African Americans and many others as well. These incidents have launched a dialogue on the topic of whether—and to what extent—black lives matter in the United States of America. The Black Lives Matter movement has given hope to many African Americans who have often been told in different ways that their lives don't matter—that, despite our coun-try's highest aspirations, they are not equal in the eyes of others.

Our country's racial divide is evidenced in part by how some have responded to the Black Lives Matter movement, specifically those who have countered with the slogan, "All Lives Matter." As noted at the beginning of this chapter, no good person can dispute the affirmation that all lives matter. In American culture, it ought to be, as the Declaration's signers put it, "self-evident." But the use of the slogan as a response to Black Lives Matter dilutes the meaning and significance of the Black Lives Matter movement. It does so by suggesting there is no need for a movement or dialogue focused specifically on the challenges African American people face in our country. This subtly suggests that black people are treated the same as everyone else.

So why the protests?

Why the complaining?

Their situation is no different from anyone else's, so why the need for a movement?

Simply stated: *All lives can't matter until black lives matter.*

Our opposition to the clearly implied message of the "All Lives Matter" response is simply, "True, all lives matter, *but* we have to wake up to the reality that our country remains divided over issues related to race. We have to own up to the fact that African Americans and other ethnic minorities in our country are mistreated far more often than most of us care to admit. Along with this, we must acknowledge that not all the problems minority groups face are the result of white racism and that some have been too quick to cite racism as the sole cause of their struggles, thus avoiding or downplaying the role of personal responsibility."

Where does all this take us? It gets us on the journey of treating all people like their lives matter. It takes us to a place in which we all have a lot to learn. A place that demands we listen more carefully to the experiences, perspectives, and feelings of others. A place we need to approach with humility and an openness to change. For some, this might be an unfamiliar place; for others not so much. But it's a place where we all need to be if we want to change things for the better.

No book has all the answers; certainly this one doesn't. It's only a start. This is not an easy journey but it is an important one. We invite you to come along.

2

Listening to Others' Stories and Sharing Our Own

One of the most important messages of this book is that if we are going to make progress with regard to behaving as if all lives matter, we need to make a genuine effort to understand others and the realities and struggles they face. The challenge is to go beyond knowing another person's reality to feeling it to the full extent that we can. We do this by listening to their stories and by sharing our own. I (John) encourage you to do this with as many others as you can.

Following is a summary of my story, along with my perspectives on some of the issues our country is facing with regard to the topic at hand.

At this writing, I am eighty-six years old. I've lived a life full of both intense sorrow and struggle as well as great happiness and joy. And I'm not done yet. At eighty-six, I know that I have been created in the image of God. And I know that my life matters. In fact, I know now that my life has always mattered. But I have not always felt that it did.

My earliest memories are of running around in a house full of aunts and cousins. When I cried out, "Mama, Mama," my cousins told me my mother was dead. So from my earliest days, I was aware that I did not have a mother. I would later learn that she died when I was just seven months old. She died in poverty, essentially of malnutrition. She was still breastfeeding me at the time of her death. I've often felt that I took the energy and nutrition she needed to survive. I don't know for sure if that is true, but I do know that she died and I lived.

I understood that I didn't have a family—an institution of affirmation and support. I didn't have a mother to love me and there was a leaky hole in my heart. As a child, I never really quite got that hole filled. I could have been angry and bitter. I could have been hardened to the point where I felt that my life didn't matter and that I could just kill myself. I could have decided that no one else's life mattered either.

Acts of kindness, like the lady from up the street who brought a quart of fresh milk to my grandmother's house for me every morning, helped affirm me as a person. My life mattered to her.

My father was still alive but he had married someone else. He and his wife lived about fifty miles away and had no children. It seemed to me that she probably liked it that way. They lived in what would be considered slaves' quarters—a one-room house behind a plantation-style home. Some of these houses can still be found today in New Hebron, where I grew up.

My father and I had a strange kind of relationship. From time to time, I would visit him and his wife, and he also would visit me at my grandmother's, usually coming alone. When I was seven years old, my grandmother and I went to visit him and in the afternoon my father and I went to buy some food for the next morning. I already knew how to write my name. So, when we went into the little grocery store to get some food and my father signed his name with an X, I was shocked.

Sometimes people who grow up with certain disadvantages in life blame other people, including their parents. But I could not blame my mother for dying when I was a baby, nor could I point a finger at my father for not knowing how to read or write. I sensed early on that I had to take responsibility for my own life.

A Lesson Learned Hauling Hay

When I was about twelve years old, I was away from home with a friend for a little summer getaway. We needed to find some work in order to make a little money so we could prove to the kids back home that we'd been away on vacation. It wasn't too hard for young people to find work because this was during World War II; a lot of the men had gone away to war. My friend and I landed a job hauling hay for a white gentleman. We knew that the going rate for a whole day of hauling hay was at least a dollar, maybe as much as a dollar and a half. We worked hard all day and then went in to get paid. Because we were black, we had to go in through the kitchen to collect our pay. I still remember how disappointed and angry I was when the gentleman handed each of us a dime and a buffalo nickel.

I was so upset that I didn't even want to take the money. I wanted to throw it on the ground because I knew the time and energy I'd put forth that day was worth far more than 15 cents. And my dignity was also worth more than that 15 cents. But despite all that, I took the money. I knew that back in those days, had I not accepted it I would have been considered a "smart, uppity nigger." The people who were raising me would have been accused of tolerating a "little smart nigger boy" who rebelled against white folk.

This incident ended up being a turning point in my life. I took responsibility for getting myself into the situation of working for that man that day. It started me to thinking: this man had the mule and he had the wagon. He had the hay and he had the field and he had the means of production. He had the capital—and I could see, even as a young boy, that the person who controlled the capital made all the decisions.

Instead of becoming bitter, I came to understand that I had value. I would take responsibility for myself and my work. I had to find a way to get the mule, the wagon, the hay, and the field. I had to take the initiative to develop whatever skills and abilities were needed to produce some combination of goods and services to improve my station in life. From that point on, I didn't wait around for anybody to offer me a job. I took the lead and I became a businessman. I wanted to contribute something of value and I wanted to learn. And I made it my responsibility to do both.

I believe that people are often pierced to the soul by how others treat them. We have to create an environment where the soul can be satisfied, or at least soothed, in its longing to be perceived as meaningful. Others in our lives balance our perspectives. When our souls cry out for significance, the pain has to be resolved.

Third-Grade Education

Because we were sharecroppers, we learned to work the fields. That was the focus; our education was not a priority. School for us was from December to January, like every other poor family of sharecroppers. I dropped out of school around the third grade, and I have lived the rest of my life trying to get an education any way possible. I have refused to be the victim of a poor education, even though people who show they are not interested in my opinion due to my lack of formal education clearly indicate that they think my life does not matter. Even today, I can sense when people disregard me based on my education and color.

I love to read even though it has come hard for me over the years. When I was young, I discovered that curiosity and hard pondering about life's issues would help me compensate for my lack of education. I love to think deeply about problems and struggles in our society. Often when I feel a burden, I begin to think, read, and talk to people about this burden. Then I usually begin to preach and teach out of this burden. This has become my education.

In other words, I take what I know about a problem and subdue it through researching, preaching, and teaching. There's always a solution. We just have to resolve to get to it.

A Brother Killed by Police

My brother Clyde served our country in World War II to help end the reign of the racist Adolph Hitler. He was honorably discharged from the military and came home decorated with ribbons to prove it. About six months after he returned, Clyde and his girlfriend, Elma, were waiting in a long line with other blacks for the movie theater ticket booth to open (whites got their tickets at a separate booth in another area of the theater). The crowd was a bit noisy, and the deputy sheriff had instructed everyone more than once to be quiet. Clyde and Elma, who were turned away from the sheriff, were talking when the officer clubbed Clyde over the head. Clyde instinctively turned and caught the club. The policeman then backed up a few steps, pulled out his gun, and shot Clyde two times in the stomach. The local doctor tried to tend to his wounds, but what he could do was limited. So my family carefully placed Clyde into my cousin's '41 Chevy and headed to the nearest hospital, which was fifty miles away in Jackson. He died that night. I remember the long ride to the hospital. I can still see him and hear him just groaning and groaning in pain. I placed my hand on his head, trying to express my love for him, but he pushed it away. I could not understand why. Perhaps he thought his life didn't matter.

After Clyde was killed, some of the white people in the community thought that black folk were going to rebel, and several black people knew what they were thinking. And perhaps people also thought that since Clyde was my brother, I would be the one to organize some kind of plot. So if I would try to join a conversation in the community, some of the black people would be afraid the white folk would see them talking with me and would just turn away.

A Life-Changing Experience in the Rankin County Jail

In February 1970, I went to the Rankin County Jail in Brandon to visit nineteen Tougaloo College students who had been volunteering with us and then had gotten arrested on their way back to Jackson following a protest march. I was subsequently arrested and tortured by white police officers. They took me inside and hit me till my blood was pouring out on the floor, then ordered me to mop up my own blood. The torture I endured that night included having a fork jammed up my nose.

It was there, on the concrete floor of the Rankin County Jail, that I truly realized the poison of racism. I saw for the first time the extent of the damage that racism had done to white people. And in the end, I felt broken. But the turning point that night came not as a result of what I saw in these white people but rather of what I saw in myself.

On that night, I witnessed the evil of racism and experienced the full force of what it could do. At first I viewed those white people as deranged animals—maggots in a bowl. If an atomic grenade had been available to me, I would have pulled the pin and thrown it at them. But then a moment came when I feared what I saw in myself and what I was capable of doing. I felt that if I responded with violence, I was no better than they were. I came face-to-face with the truth that we are all broken, and that the solution was not violence or retaliation but love.

In my brokenness, I said to God, "If you get me out of this jail, I will preach your love and your gospel in a way that allows me to claim forgiveness but also in a way that allows me to forgive those who did this to me." Remembering God's grace in forgiving me for my own sins helped me find a place of forgiveness even in that heinous situation.

It was clear to me that things in our society would change. They had to. More and more, we black people were coming to the realization that our lives mattered, and we were not going to retreat from this understanding. But I was also committed, by God's grace, to achieving the goal of true freedom through peaceful means based on my belief that all lives mattered and that all people—even the oppressors—bear the image of God.

I have many of the characteristics of people often written off as unimportant, people who often come to feel that their lives do not matter. I grew up with no mother, with no father in my home, with little education, in poverty, and with a brother killed by law enforcement because he was too loud. These circumstances could have caused me to grow up believing that my life did not matter. Yet, by the grace of God and many caring people, I know today that my life does matter. Mutual love for one another demonstrates that all lives matter. That is what the church ought to be about: demonstrating care and concern for others, bearing each other's pain. The apostle Paul preached this message (Gal. 6:2).

Advancing the message that all lives matter is what I've committed my life to and it is what I want to live the rest of my life doing. My favorite song lyrics are from a children's song: "Jesus loves the little children, all the children of the world. Red, brown, yellow, black, and white, they are precious in his sight." It's a simple message but a profound one—one that should be at the center of all our thoughts and actions. For we are *all* God's children and we are *all* precious in his sight. So, as terrifying as my experience in the Rankin County Jail was, I am forever grateful that it put me on the path of reconciliation and that I've remained on it all these many years.

———————

The other day I ran into a young black teenager who was despondent. He had a gun and was acting like a loose cannon running down the street. I grabbed him and began to talk with him. He had all the characteristics of a young gangbanger. He told me that he already had given up on life and did not care about what happened to himself, or anyone else for that matter. He had been told in numerous ways by society that his life did not matter. He was primed to kill someone and ready to turn the gun on himself. I told him that his life did matter. I told him of God's love for him. Somehow we have to find ways to reach out to these young boys who are shooting, to let them know that their lives do matter.

This is not to say that people who are being oppressed or treated as if their lives don't matter should be passive. In keeping with Benjamin Mays's book *Born to Rebel*, I think that God created human beings to be free and to rebel against oppression. There is no attribute of God that can be cited to justify one person oppressing another. But when we take our stand, we must do so peacefully. Otherwise we risk becoming the enemy.

All people need to accept responsibility for improving the society in which we live. We need to work together to create a climate that clearly acknowledges that all lives matter. All people have inherent dignity but many don't know it, feel it, or believe it. Hurting people often turn to violence, drugs, gangs, and other destructive behavior as a remedy for their pain. They view themselves as victims. But when they come to understand and believe that their lives matter, they will take responsibility for their own lives and show concern for the lives of others. They need help to do this.

Because their pain is real, I believe it can only be soothed through real forgiveness and reconciliation. When people are angry, their souls cry out for relief. They might conclude, *I'll just kill myself,* or *I'll just kill somebody else.* For them life doesn't matter, and this mindset affects people of every culture and ethnicity. Even in America, we have documented cases where hurting people turned to massive violence in our schools, movie theaters, and even churches.

The neglected soul does not have to lead to violence but it must have expression. For Muddy Waters, it was the blues. The soul must have expression; it cannot be satisfied with fame, prosperity, or other worldly attributes. Everyone has a soul. The soul is the dignity of human life.

"And the LORD God formed man of the dust of the ground, and breathed into his nostrils the breath of life; and man became a living soul" (Gen. 2:7 KJV). All lives matter to God!

So where do we go from here? The apostle Paul said, "Carry each other's burdens, and in this way you will fulfill the law of Christ" (Gal. 6:2). Somehow, it all comes down to mutual love and respect for one another. Period. We must have enough love to reach out and feel the pain of others, bear it in ourselves, and look to Christ for resolution. As the called-out ones—the body of Christ, the church—we should be the model for that.

3

Owning Up

A Candid Overview of US History

Most have heard the quote, "Those who cannot remember the past are condemned to repeat it." It comes from the 1905 book *The Life of Reason* by George Santayana. But there is at least one other important reason to know history: we can't fully understand who we are without understanding who we have been.

We need to move beyond the idea that a critical evaluation of our country's past (and its present, for that matter) means we are anti-American or unpatriotic. We can be proud of our country and its many positive features and noble ideals while still pointing out where we as a nation have come up short or been plainly wrong. Consider that Thomas Jefferson, author of the Declaration of Independence, once stated, "I tremble for my country when I reflect that God is just: that his justice cannot sleep forever."*

*Thomas Jefferson, "Query XVIII," *Notes on the State of Virginia*, ed. William Peden (Chapel Hill: University of North Carolina Press, 1955), 163.

As noted earlier, our country's founding declaration states that all men are created equal. Life, liberty, and the pursuit of happiness are core features of the American identity. Our national anthem makes reference to "the land of the free." But it's obvious that from the very beginning some were freer and more equal than others.

Clearly women were not equal to men. It took our country nearly 150 years for women just to gain the right to vote, which is fundamental to a democratic society. Even after gaining this right as a result of the Nineteenth Amendment, adopted in 1920, women were a long way from achieving full equality. It's also clear that the Founding Fathers did not count the indigenous peoples of this land as human beings who were equal in the sight of God. The Declaration of Independence refers to Native Americans as "merciless Indian savages." And, of course, slaves brought to this country against their will were regarded essentially as subhuman. They were not persons; they were property that could be bought and sold.

I (Wayne) cannot help but consider what this means to me personally. Anne, who is my wife—my life partner and soulmate—was not included. My good friend Mark Charles, a Native American, was not included. My best friend and longtime mentor John Perkins was not included. To the signers of the Declaration of Independence, none of their lives mattered.

Native Americans

Imagine how Native Americans over the years might have felt about their lives and how much they matter. At the end of the fifteenth century, people from Europe began arriving in the Americas. They mislabeled the natives "Indians" because they thought they had sailed to India, and essentially considered this new land theirs for the taking. It didn't matter to them that people were already living here. The newcomers claimed the land as their own and systematically began taking it over. This pattern continued for the next three hundred years, until virtually all native inhabitants were either eliminated or confined. Their lives didn't matter.

To grasp this reality, imagine that you have invited a few people to your house for dinner, and afterward they decide to stay. They spend the night and then proceed to invite other family members to your house to stay for a while. As the days go by, they remain and eventually begin taking over your home. Soon you are isolated—confined to an upstairs bedroom while the rest of your house is occupied by foreigners, people you don't even know. How would you feel?

It's estimated that when Columbus hit the shores of the Americas there were between seven and fifteen million natives living in the land. By the dawn of the twentieth century, according to estimates, the number had declined to fewer than three hundred thousand. In other words, an entire people group had largely been wiped out. Diseases brought from the Old World—small pox, measles, and others—were partly to blame, as natives were unable to tolerate them. Of course there were also massacres and declared wars against Native Americans. And as will be discussed in greater detail in chapter 6, Europeans did what they did to Native Americans with the full blessing of the church.

The Native Americans who gave up the fight were relocated to reservations, where they have been treated at best as second-class citizens. In dealing with the indigenous people of the land, the US government has signed and broken more than five hundred treaties, something perfectly acceptable if one agrees to the premise that some lives don't matter much, if at all.

My friend Mark Charles, mentioned above, has been outspoken about the mistreatment of his people over the centuries. He has been a part of several Christian Community Development Association (CCDA) conferences and has led several CCDA workshops over the years. Mark spent the better part of a year spreading the word about his plan to go to the Capitol steps and read an apology—just a few short sentences—that the American government had made to Native Americans. This formal apology was inserted by Senator Sam Brownback into House Resolution 3326, Department of Defense Appropriations Act, and buried on page 45 in sub-section 8113.

The bill passed and went to President Obama's desk to be signed on December 19, 2009. The signing of this bill was private and there was no press conference regarding it. The White House did issue a press release about the bill but no mention was made of the apology contained within it. Not many even knew of its existence and it had never been read publicly.

My son Austin, who has a special interest in reconciliation with Native Americans, came with me to Washington, DC, for the fifth anniversary of this bill's signing on December 19, 2014, to hear the public reading of this apology. Despite Mark's promotional efforts, only about two hundred people gathered on the Capitol lawn that day. Although the turnout was disappointing, it was a moving experience for those who did come.

Do all lives matter? Yes, but we have treated Native Americans as if their lives don't.

African Americans

If you have never seen a slave ship, we recommend you use Google to check out what one looked like. A stained glass window at the New Mount Pilgrim Missionary Baptist Church in Chicago, where our good friend Marshall Hatch is senior pastor, features a prominent depiction of a slave ship. It portrays the grossly unsanitary conditions suggestive of the cruel and inhumane treatment of those who came to America as slaves.

The entertainment industry has, from time to time, provided the public with a glimpse of what it was like to come over on a slave ship. Examples include the 1970s TV miniseries *Roots* and the Steven Spielberg movie *Amistad*. We recommend that you read up on the realities of this so-called Middle Passage. It's one thing to know about it; it's quite another to truly understand and feel what it was like for people, something we cannot do completely.

Of course, once these Africans arrived in America they were routinely whipped or beaten in other ways. They could be hanged if they caused too much trouble. Some masters were kinder than others but all of them considered their slaves as property.

It's almost incomprehensible to consider how poorly some human beings treated other human beings during the slavery era. Yet it's easier to understand when considering that slaves were not regarded as being fully human. Our US Constitution considered a slave three-fifths of a person. Obviously, if someone is only three-fifths of a person, his or her life doesn't matter that much.

The American economy, especially in the South, grew richer and richer because of the labor of people who had no choice but to work for free, and it was all done under the banner of white supremacy.

The path to freedom for slaves took a major step forward with Lincoln's Emancipation Proclamation on January 1, 1863. In 1865, the Thirteenth Amendment was passed, stating that "neither slavery nor involuntary servitude, except for as a punishment for crime whereof the party shall have been duly convicted, shall exist within the United States, or anyplace subject to their jurisdiction." In other words, slavery was abolished in the United States.

Three years later, the Fourteenth Amendment granted citizenship to "all persons born or naturalized in the United States." This included former slaves who'd been recently freed. This amendment also forbade states from denying any person "life, liberty or property, without due process of law" or to "deny to any person within its jurisdiction the equal protection of the laws." Thus the Fourteenth Amendment greatly expanded the protection of civil rights to all Americans. The intent of the Declaration of Independence was finally realized.

Then, in 1870, came the Fifteenth Amendment, which stated that "the right of citizens of the United States to vote shall not be denied or abridged by the United States or by any state on the account of race, color or previous condition of servitude." Technically, now all males, including African Americans and Native Americans, were given the right to vote.

But freedom on paper did not mean freedom in reality. Not by a long shot. Among many other things, various tricks and techniques were regularly practiced to keep people from voting. The government promised former slaves forty acres and a mule—in other words, a fresh start in life. But these proposed reparations never came about. In the Reconstruction period that followed the Civil War, many African Americans began doing quite well, even owning their own land and serving in government positions, including as elected officials. In fact they were doing so well that a whole new system had to be put in place to hold them down, a system that became known as Jim Crow. With Jim Crow, state and local laws that treated black people as inferior ruled the day for a hundred years after slavery ended.

The Jim Crow era witnessed the emergence of the Ku Klux Klan and other white supremacy organizations, leading to countless beatings and killings, including hangings, of black people, many of whom lived in constant fear, especially in the South, where "Whites Only" signs became prominent in public places. African Americans were American enough to fight for their country in wars but at home did not have access to the very freedoms for which they fought. This blatant hypocrisy came to an end with the American Civil Rights movement, specifically the adoption of the Civil Rights Act of 1964 and the Voting Rights Act of 1965.

Once again, however, these legislative acts brought full equality to black people only on paper. Making it illegal to discriminate based on race did not bring about an end to racial discrimination. Michelle Alexander makes this case in her book *The New Jim*

Crow, which is a must-read for anyone wanting to understand what it is like to be black in America today. Features of the New Jim Crow include the mass incarceration of African Americans and the war on young African American men (under the guise of a war on drugs) playing out on the street corners in cities across America. To anyone who enters a courtroom in one of our cities, it should be obvious who has the power and who does not. Almost all of those who have been charged with a crime are people of color, while the overwhelming majority of judges, states attorneys, and lawyers are white. Based on the courtrooms of our urban criminal justice system, it certainly appears as if the lives of people of color don't matter.

According to an old adage often repeated by the people of Lawndale, "If you're white, you're all right; if you're brown, stick around; but if you're black, get back." The adage is justified. The University of Chicago does a regular study focused on prejudice in America, and every time it does, researchers reach the same conclusion—the darker your skin color, the more you will be the victim of discrimination. Bad news—but not surprising news—for African Americans, who have been told regularly and in many different ways that their lives don't matter.

The overwhelming majority of African Americans have personally experienced discrimination. In July 2016, Senator Tim Scott of South Carolina, the only black Republican in the Senate, delivered a moving speech on the Senate floor describing how he had been stopped by law enforcement seven times in just the past year apparently for no other reason than driving a nice car in the wrong neighborhood, a phenomenon commonly referred to as "driving while black." Our good friend Noel Castellanos, the president of CCDA, visited Flint, Michigan, in the summer of 2016. He confirmed that the unsanitary water there was confined mostly to the poor African American areas of town. The drinking water was fine in areas where white people live.

Final Thoughts

Throughout history, some human beings have treated other human beings as if their lives didn't matter. African Americans, Native Americans, and women have not been the only victims of prejudice. In the United States during World War II, Japanese American citizens were automatically considered the enemy and sent to work camps. In the past, the Catholic Church has faced intense discrimination from the culture at large. Today, Mexican immigrants, peace-loving Muslims, and the LGBTQ community are among the groups who face discrimination. Poor people—regardless of ethnicity, gender, or sexual orientation—are always at risk of being marginalized. And although many think of the white middle class as the only demographic that steers clear of discrimination, even white males might feel mistreated when they are passed over for a job or admission to a college as a result of affirmative action policies that work to their disadvantage.

We live in a complicated world in which people sometimes disagree when it comes to determining what is fair and right in individual situations or with regard to public policy. But it behooves all of us to strive toward higher levels of understanding of and compassion for others.

This chapter has focused on women, Native Americans, and African Americans because of our view that so many in our culture underestimate the extent to which all three groups still face an uphill battle. We can and should celebrate the progress we have made with women's rights, thanks in part to lobbying groups such as the National Organization for Women. The treatment of women in the United States stands as a model for much of the rest of the world, where in some places women are still treated essentially as property. But even in America—based on factors such as how much they are paid for doing the same jobs as men and how they are treated in the workplace and in other settings—many women still feel like their lives don't matter. As for Native Americans, many are still paying the price for how this country has treated them in the past.

Of course, John and I are intimately familiar with the reality faced by African Americans. It's frustrating to hear white people make statements such as, "Slavery was a long time ago, so get over it," or "We live in a post-racial society; we even have a black president, so what more do you want?"

Or, "It's time for black people to take responsibility for their own lives."

Yes, African American people—as all people—ought to take personal responsibility for making the right choices, even in the midst of an uphill battle. But this is easier said than done. To relegate the slavery era and subsequent generations of racist legal and social policies to the past is not just logically absurd but is at the least insensitive if not immoral. Centuries of discrimination continue to shape the lives and limit the choices of African American people in our country today.

Benjamin Watson writes that "white people have no idea of the fear that black people feel toward the police. I cannot say that strongly enough, loudly enough, or forcefully enough. Black people have little expectation of being treated fairly by police in any situation."* Watson voiced this view after having been picked up near a hospital in the middle of the night by a police officer for no apparent reason. Another case of driving while black.

As a white male, as I read about our country's history, I find it difficult to come to grips with how white men have been able to systematically dominate our culture. And I must admit that at times I feel embarrassed upon realizing my unmerited privilege. Which is why I want to do what I can to build the case that all lives matter and that our nation cannot turn a blind eye to the blight of racial prejudice in our past or our present.

*Benjamin Watson, *Under Our Skin* (Wheaton, IL: Tyndale, 2015), 91.

4

Invisible People

Often when we think of contemporary expressions of racism or sexism we think of obvious things such as unjustified and unnecessary police shootings, persons of color getting stiffer sentences for the same crimes, or women not receiving equal pay for equal work. But discrimination also has a subtler side. This subtler side reveals its face—often unintentionally—when we don't notice the people around us. In effect they become invisible, and to the extent that they go unheard and unnoticed, they get the message that their lives don't matter.

On a number of occasions Anne and I found ourselves in the company of a woman who loved to talk about God's heart for the poor, racial discrimination, and various other social topics. It seemed as if every time we talked, this woman turned her back on Anne and spoke to me only, even though Anne had as much to contribute to the conversation as I did. One time, after this happened yet again, Anne said to me upon getting home that night, "When I'm with her, I feel like I don't matter. I feel unimportant; it's like I'm not even there. I feel invisible." Anne went on to say that she doubted this woman even knew her name, even though they had been together dozens of times.

I have had similar experiences when having conversations with white leaders when some of my closest African American friends and colleagues were also present. I can recall several occasions when a white person came to the church to give a presentation on one topic or another to our leadership team of Pastor Joseph Atkins; Chelsea Johnson, my executive assistant; and Pastor Darryl Saffore (all three African Americans). Almost without fail, these white visitors would look at me and ignore the others, even though most of the time at least one if not all of them knew far more than I did about the subject being discussed. The white person in the room tacitly assumes that the other white person is the decision maker and has the best understanding of the issue.

Often this dynamic is so noticeable that we are all uncomfortable, even embarrassed, for the visitor. I try to pull the others in by asking for their opinions or having them pose a question directly to the visitor. More often than not, however, even this strategy doesn't stop the white man or woman from looking at me even as they respond to someone else's question. These kinds of interactions send the message to Joe, Chelsea, and Darryl that their thoughts, comments, and opinions—in a word, their lives—don't matter.

Cross-racial encounters that send negative messages to persons of color are far more common than many people, primarily white folks, realize. Several years ago, Leroy Barber, an African American man who is now president of the Voices Project, moved to the inner city of Atlanta. One of the donors to his ministry came to visit with both Leroy and a white man who had also relocated to this inner-city community. This donor had a perfectly good heart and wanted to support the ministry. But during the meeting the donor became enamored of the white man, completely captivated and impressed that this white person had moved his family to a tough neighborhood, sending his kids to an inner-city school and putting his whole family at some risk.

Completely lost on this well-intentioned and kindhearted donor was the fact that Leroy and his wife, Donna, had done exactly the same thing as his white colleague had done. Donna and Leroy were well educated, upwardly mobile, and a much-sought-after family for leadership in the Christian community. Just like the white family, they had numerous choices of where to live but chose, based on their values and priorities, inner-city Atlanta.

Throughout the meeting, the donor looked not at Leroy (even though he was the head of the ministry) but at this white neighbor who'd also relocated. When the donor asked, "How can I help you?" he directed his question only to the white neighbor. It's as if he was asking, *How can we make sure you, white family, are being taken care of in this dangerous community?* (He even gave the white neighbor some extra money.) This donor never once asked Leroy how he and his family were doing. Again, he seemed completely oblivious to the fact that Leroy had relocated to this same community and in so doing was also putting his life and the life of his family at greater risk.

For the record, Leroy Barber's life matters greatly to John and me. He's been a colleague of ours throughout the CCDA movement and is currently serving as chair of the CCDA board. I recall having a conversation with him shortly after the incident described above. He expressed disappointment and hurt at receiving the message—unintended though it may have been—that his life and the lives of his family didn't matter as much as the lives of others. Unfortunately, many white people have grown up in a culture that almost innately thinks that black people have very little to contribute to a conversation. It is this unconscious learned behavior that is frequently picked up by African Americans and other people of color, telling them that their lives don't matter.

And then there is the young African American doctor from Chicago who recently began a residency in the Boston area. On his first day on the job at the hospital, he was sitting at a table when someone walked up to him and asked if he was the new janitor. Not long after that he went to surgery, all decked out in surgical scrubs. But as he approached the doctor performing the surgery, the attending nurse asked quietly, to the lead physician, "Who is this guy and why is he here?" The nurse looked dumbfounded upon learning that this young black man would be participating in the surgery. Instead of having the positive experience he had expected, the young doctor stood somewhere between demeaned and mortified.

It's not just everyday conversations and routine interactions that reveal the presence of invisible people. In early July 2016, the nation experienced one of its most tense and wrenching times as on consecutive days African American men were shot and killed by police, first in Baton Rouge, Louisiana, and then just outside St. Paul, Minnesota. A few days later, five Dallas police officers were shot and killed by a black man in apparent retaliation.

But even as the nation was mourning, my heart turned to my own community. In the same period of just a few days that spanned the killings of Alton Sterling, Philando Castile, and the five Dallas police officers, 114 people were shot in Chicago. Eleven of them died. The nation's attention was focused on the five Dallas police officers who'd been killed and their families. They got lots of publicity, even a special address from the president, something that was right and good. Yet no one seemed to care about those 114 people—especially the eleven who lost their lives—in Chicago. Where was the mourning for them? In fact, most of these incidents didn't even make the local news. This ought to make us wonder how much the lives of people on the South and West Sides of Chicago, especially Americans of African descent, truly matter.

One of my first lessons regarding invisible people still haunts me today. It came in the 1970s during my first year as a teacher at Farragut High School on the West Side. An African American teen in my class had become one of my prize students. We knew him by his nickname, "Top Cat." He did his homework faithfully, came to class every day, earned straight As, was always front and center, and was willing and able to answer almost any question. But then one day, Top Cat didn't show up to class. I waited for a few minutes before finally asking, "Does anyone know anything about Top Cat?"

A few students responded, "Coach, you didn't hear?"

To which I replied, "Hear what?"

They proceeded to tell me that there'd been a holdup at the gas station where Top Cat worked at night, and that he had been shot dead.

I remember that day like it was yesterday. I especially remember trying to go to Top Cat's funeral, but I couldn't even find out where it was. No newspaper, no TV or radio newscast, nothing anywhere about the death of Top Cat. He was one of those nameless and faceless people about whom nobody seems to care and whose life doesn't seem to matter.

Invisible.

The star of our class had simply gone out.

5

Building on Common Ground

On Sunday morning, July 10, 2016, I was in the midst of my summer study leave from Lawndale Community Church and Anne and I decided to attend St. Paul & the Redeemer Episcopal Church, an ethnically integrated church in a multicultural community near the University of Chicago on the city's South Side. We'd never been there before.

Immediately upon entering, we felt welcomed and at home. No doubt this was largely because we saw several people of color. This was not a white church; it was an integrated church, one that had worked hard to establish genuine community, in part by celebrating diverse ethnicities and experiences. There was a baptism that morning as well as communion. Both felt friendly, open, and welcoming. Pastor Peter Lane said the communion table was open to all, and this invitation genuinely helped Anne and me to worship the Lord that morning even in the midst of the stress we were feeling about what the nation was going through.

But it was Pastor Lane's message that touched our hearts most deeply. The first words out of his mouth were, "Philando Castile was a thirty-two-year-old cafeteria supervisor at a St. Paul school and a respected member of his union. He was killed by the police for being black." *Wow!* He had our full attention. The pastor continued, "Alton Sterling was a thirty-seven-year-old roving CD salesman with five children. He had criminal convictions that perhaps forced him into the informal economy used by so many whom employers turn aside. He was killed by the police for being black."

Immediately I sensed that this white Episcopal priest had an understanding that comes only from experience—only from being part of a church that is intentionally multiracial and multicultural. Peter Lane understood the depth of the problem. Later in his sermon he quoted Minnesota Governor Dayton, who had said that, were Castile white, he would still be alive.

The pastor urged solidarity with the Black Lives Matter movement. But he didn't stop there. He then delved into the killing of five Dallas police officers by a sniper with an assault rifle, officers who were doing one of the most American things a police officer can do: protecting people who were protesting peacefully. The pastor went on to say that the events of the past week had brought focus to the bedrock of racism that underlies our country and the roots of fear that infiltrate our culture. He stressed the importance of understanding the depth of the problems and issues we were facing while clearly condemning *all* violence.

After leaving the church in Hyde Park, Anne and I felt we needed to go to our home church. We quickly made our way to Lawndale, where the challenging task of addressing a congregation that was feeling the pain of recent events fell to our associate pastor, Joseph Atkins. Pastor Joe was the perfect person to answer the call. He was one of the high school boys who had helped give birth to Lawndale Community Church, and he'd had several negative experiences with police officers. On one occasion when he was harassed, I intervened with the district commander. Joe, along with me and many others at Lawndale, has buried far too many people who have been killed in our community.

Anne and I sat in the back of church and could not keep from smiling as we realized that Joe was saying exactly what needed to be said. He talked about the struggles of being a black man in America. But while affirming the black men in our church and their right to be upset about the recent police shootings of two more black men, he also condemned the violence in Dallas.

"I am a black man," he said, "and I am not to be feared. Please don't be afraid of me because I am black." He went on to state that every drop of blood is precious in God's sight, no matter what the color of a person's skin. He quoted Psalm 72, which states that righteousness and justice must work together in our communities if our society is to be sustainable and fair for all. From our perspective, Joe had hit a home run. I can't remember a day when I've been prouder to be associated with Lawndale Community Church.

But I wasn't done going to church. My daughter, Angela, who'd been with us at Lawndale, and I then decided to go to New Mount Pilgrim Missionary Baptist Church to hear what Pastor Marshall Hatch had to say. The church was hosting a unity prayer service that afternoon and had invited people of all ethnicities to come. At this gathering, Pastor Hatch made it abundantly clear that all lives matter, that every life is precious. He echoed the themes of both Pastor Lane and Pastor Joe, condemning all violence while also pointing out that there were many people in our country who had been made to feel like their lives don't matter.

Two days later, on July 12, President Obama went to Dallas along with former president George W. Bush and his wife, Vice President Biden and his wife, the mayor of Dallas, and many others to attend a memorial service for the fallen police officers. It was a tough day; it's always hard when people who have devoted their lives to serving and protecting citizens are killed in the line of duty. It seemed that all of America, not just Dallas, was grieving.

I was not able to see the whole service, but was particularly interested in what President Obama had to say after several people told me they considered it one of his best speeches ever. So I got a copy of the speech from the White House Press Office.*

> I know that Americans are struggling right now with what we've witnessed over the past week. First, the shootings in Minnesota and Baton Rouge, and the protests, then the targeting of police by the shooter here—an act not just of demented violence but of racial hatred. All of it has left us wounded, and angry, and hurt. It's as if the deepest fault lines of our democracy have suddenly been exposed, perhaps even widened. And although we know that such divisions are not new—though they have surely been worse in even the recent past—that offers us little comfort.

In that short paragraph, President Obama captured the pulse of the American society. We have a racial divide, yet we mourn—and we mourn together. The president continued:

> Faced with this violence, we wonder if the divides of race in America can ever be bridged. We wonder if an African-American community that feels unfairly targeted by police, and police departments that feel unfairly maligned for doing their jobs, can ever understand each other's experience. . . . We see all this, and it's hard not to think sometimes that the center won't hold and that things might get worse.

These words make total sense to the people of Lawndale, who feel this tension on a regular basis. Police are here to serve and protect and yet there are some—a minority—of police who use their badges to live out their biases and prejudices. And then there are some, including the shooter in Dallas, who decide to take advantage of the moment.

*"Remarks by the President at Memorial Service for Fallen Dallas Police Officers," July 12, 2016, https://www.whitehouse.gov/the-press-office/2016/07/12/remarks-president-memorial-service-fallen-dallas-police-officers.

The president offered hope:

> I understand. I understand how Americans are feeling. But, Dallas, I am here to say we must reject such despair. I'm here to insist that we are not as divided as we seem. And I know that because I know America. I know how far we have come against impossible odds. I know we'll make it because of what I've experienced in my own life, what I've seen in this country and its people—their goodness and decency—as President of the United States. And I know it because of what we've seen here in Dallas—how all of you, out of great suffering, have shown us the meaning of perseverance and character, and hope.

Near the end of his address, President Obama drew from the Old Testament book of Ezekiel: "I will give you a new heart, the Lord says, and put a new spirit in you. I will remove from you your heart of stone and give you a heart of flesh." Then he elaborated: "A new heart. Not a heart of stone, but a heart open to the fears and hopes and challenges of our fellow citizens. That's what we must sustain." In other words, a heart that recognizes that all lives matter.

Hannah Buchanan is an assistant pastor of outreach at Highland Park United Methodist, a Dallas megachurch, where they lit five candles on Sunday morning for the five Dallas police officers. A couple days later, Hannah wrote a blog post that raised some profound questions.† "If you were there this weekend, you remember we lit five tall candles and many more tea lights at the base. We chose to light five in honor of the Dallas Police Officers who were tragically killed in *our* city." But then Buchanan wrote, "I wonder though, should we have lit seven?" I stopped cold after that sentence.

She went on to ask, "When did the story start for you?" She questions whether it was when the Dallas police officers were shot on July 7, or earlier when Alton Sterling and Philando Castile

---

†Hannah Buchanan, "Five Candles or Seven," HPUMC, July 12, 2016, http://www.hpumc.org/about-us/stories/five-candles-or-seven/.

were shot and killed? Or did it start when Trayvon Martin was shot and killed? Or did it start when Michael Brown was shot and killed? Or with American slavery? Or Jim Crow laws? Or did it start when the Civil Rights legislation was passed but didn't solve all our problems?

Pastor Lane's message, Pastor Joe Atkins's sermon, President Obama's address, and Hannah Buchanan's blog post all have something extremely important in common: none of them take sides. Often it seems the media, including social media, want to turn our nation's struggles into a kind of war between the Black Lives Matter movement and law enforcement officials or between so-called liberals and conservatives. But these four people refused to fall into that trap. Instead, they recognized pain, acknowledged suffering wherever it was, and advocated for peace, compassion, and understanding, not retaliation and violence.

It was in December 2014 when I walked into the Green Tomato Café in Chicago and found James Brooks, senior pastor of Harmony Community Church in Chicago, looking bewildered. "Coach," he asked, "what are we going to do about it?" He was asking about what we might do about the non-indictment of the police officer in New York City who was responsible for the choking death of Eric Garner. In some circles there had been a call for churches to stage some kind of demonstration to voice disagreement with the lack of charges being brought against the police officer.

James and I decided our churches would join forces. We quickly came up with a plan. At 11:15 a.m. on Sunday, the people of Harmony Community Church and Lawndale Community Church would walk out of our respective services together onto Ogden Avenue. We would walk quietly but with the clear intention to disrupt the morning traffic as we occupied the corner of Central Park and Ogden Avenue. After marching for justice, we would hold hands in solidarity, block all traffic in the intersection, and pray for justice and peace.

We spread the word of our plan to our congregations through email and texting. At Lawndale, our 8:30 service went on as normal. At 11:00, we briefly shared before walking out into the streets. The police were aware of our plan and had stated that they would arrest us if we disrupted traffic. Anne and I were the first to leave the church. The chair of our deacon board, Thomas Worthy, along with his wife, Tracie, and others from our pastoral team also helped lead the way.

About eight hundred people from Lawndale Community Church and another 150 from Harmony Community Church walked out onto the streets that December day. People from other churches—Lawndale Christian Reformed Church, River City Community Church, New Life Community Church, Little Village Community Church, and others—joined in. Helicopters flew overhead to monitor our actions or record them for the media. Later we discovered that we were live on several local TV stations.

We chanted, "Let Justice Roll Down; Loving God, Loving People" as more than 1,200 of us walked four blocks down Ogden Avenue to a major intersection that is home to bus stops and an el train stop, not to mention heavy traffic. All of us assumed we would be arrested and detained. But lo and behold, instead of arresting us, the police joined in. Over fifty police officers blocked traffic so we could march and stood in solidarity with us, showing their opposition to police brutality. Before walking back, we shook hands with and hugged every one of them. In the middle of a busy Chicago intersection, we prayed for the police of the 10th district and the whole city of Chicago, shutting down traffic for fifteen minutes as we prayed together.

Despite the perception that one has to be on one side or the other, the overwhelming majority of people in this country—including law enforcement officials and leaders of the Black Lives Matter movement—want the same thing: peace and justice in our communities and in our nation. It's time to build on this common ground, on the foundation we share. It's time to ignore the messages of those who are intent on driving wedges between and among us. Most of all, it's time for us to strive together to proclaim the message that all lives matter and then to live this message as fully as we can.

6

Black Lives Matter

A Christian Response

If asked who in history might be considered the quintessential racist, for many the name that would come to mind is Adolph Hitler. Hitler made no apologies for his conviction that the Aryan race—which was of course the one to which he belonged—was superior. And he had no reservations about exterminating anyone and everyone who happened not to be a member of this favored race of people.

One could easily argue that Hitler had psychological or spiritual or emotional problems—or all three plus more. But viewed from a Christian perspective, whatever else he might have had, he had a fundamental theological problem.

Christians, including those who call themselves evangelicals, can and do reach different conclusions regarding how biblical principles ought to inform various moral, social, and public policy issues. Sincere people can read the same Bible and disagree on how it should be interpreted and applied in various situations and contexts.

But on some matters the Bible is abundantly clear—beyond any reasonable debate. And one of those matters is that *all* human beings are equal in the sight of God.

For convenience of communication, it's common to use the terms "race" and "racism." But according to any geneticist, there are not multiple races of humans. There is one and only one race. No matter how different the lightest-skinned person from Europe might look from the darkest-skinned person from India or Africa, our DNA is the same.

There is nothing in the Bible to suggest anything different, while there is ample support for the idea that, despite whatever differences we might have, we are all one, united and equal in our humanity. Genesis 1:27 informs us that God created human beings—male and female—in his image. Psalm 139:14–17 reads:

> I praise you because I am fearfully and wonderfully made;
>   your works are wonderful,
>   I know that full well.
> My frame was not hidden from you
>   when I was made in the secret place,
>   when I was woven together in the depths of the earth.
> Your eyes saw my unformed body;
>   all the days ordained for me were written in your book
>   before one of them came to be.
> How precious to me are your thoughts, God!
>   How vast is the sum of them!"

Scripture teaches that God, our Creator, knew each of us even when we were in our mother's womb.

Only the insidiousness of evil in our world can explain how anyone could find in Scripture justification for considering any person—let alone an entire "race" or ethnicity of people—any more or less important in God's eyes.

Hitler was not the only one who had a major theological problem. In fact, at times in its history the church had a similar problem.

It was through our Native American friend Mark Charles that we became aware of something known as the "Doctrine of Discovery." This doctrine originated in the Catholic Church through a series of papal edicts that came out in the late 1400s. It essentially provided theological justification for the Christian empire of Europe to take over any land inhabited by non-Christian people. This doctrine gave full license to explorers such as Columbus to come to the so-called New World and overthrow whomever they had to in order to take over the land. They did it with the church's blessing, believing they were doing the work of the kingdom of God, that it was God's will for them to overtake the indigenous people of the Americas and other places around the globe, including Africa.

The nineteenth-century philosophy of Manifest Destiny, according to which it was the destiny of the United States to claim and take over the continent from coast to coast, also contributed to the unjust treatment of Native Americans and spread the message that their lives did not matter.

The church throughout history has, at times, been pretty good at finding biblical support to justify immoral behavior. The majority of those who owned slaves in America were Christians. They found their theological justification mainly in Genesis 9:25–27, where, after the great flood, Noah laid a curse on Ham, "the father of Canaan," because of his indiscretion, saying "Cursed be Canaan! The lowest of slaves will he be to his brothers" (v. 25). And according to Christian tradition, the Canaanites settled in Africa. This is what justified chattel slavery in the minds of many.

How Much Has Changed?

On July 10, 2016, the Black Lives Matter activist group released the following ten-point manifesto detailing what police practices and behavior in America it would like to see changed. It includes a couple of explanatory notes, which we have provided.

1. End "broken windows" policing, which aggressively polices minor crimes in an attempt to solve larger ones. (Note: the concern here is that this kind of policing leads to the unfair targeting—including "stop and frisks"—of black men and women.)

2. Use community oversight for police misconduct rather than having the police department decide what consequences its officers should face.

3. Make standards for reporting police use of deadly force.

4. Independently investigate and prosecute police misconduct.

5. Have the racial makeup of police departments reflect the communities they serve.

6. Require officers to wear body cameras.

7. Provide more training for police officers.

8. End for-profit policing practices. (Note: as of now, police can legally confiscate money and property that they believe is in some way linked to a crime. And they can use it in any way they see fit, even if no one is ever convicted of the crime.)

9. End the police use of military equipment.

10. Implement police union contracts to hold officers accountable for misconduct.*

It's possible to quibble about a few of these proposals—and whether they would be good and feasible changes to make. But overall they are reasonable requests, rooted largely in common sense. They have nothing to do with violence or retaliation. They

*Tom Proctor, "Black Lives Matter Just Delivered Their 10 Point Manifesto, and This Is What They Want," politicsbreaking.com, July 10, 2016, http://politics breaking.com/black-lives-matter-just-delivered-10-point-manifesto-want/. See also Veronique de Rugy, "The Ten-Point Manifesto of Black Lives Matter," National Review, July 13, 2016, http://www.nationalreview.com/corner/437726/black -lives-matter-manifesto-ten-points.

are aimed simply at making community policing not only more fair but also more effective and successful.

What does the church—specifically evangelicals—think of these proposals? According to the Barna research organization, 94 percent of evangelicals believe the church plays an important role in racial reconciliation. Yet only 13 percent of evangelicals support the Black Lives Matter movement, even though many of its foundational principles are faithful to Scripture and many of its leaders and participants are Christians.

Frankly, as people who self-identify as evangelicals and who generally believe what evangelicals believe theologically, we find this statistic both disheartening and discouraging. Essentially, it sends the message, "All lives matter, but I'm not going to support a peaceful movement that is calling attention to the fact that we are still treating some people as if their lives don't matter."

We don't doubt that we've come a long way as a church and as a culture. But we also don't doubt that we still have a long way to go. One of the hallmarks of evangelical faith is taking the Bible seriously. We suggest starting by taking the lesson Jesus teaches in Luke 10 seriously. An expert in the law asks Jesus what he has to do to gain eternal life. Jesus responds with a question of his own and asks the man what he thinks. The expert replies, "'Love the Lord your God with all your heart and with all your soul and with all your strength and with all your mind'; and, 'Love your neighbor as yourself'" (v. 27).

Jesus tells the man he has answered correctly. But the expert has another question: "Who is my neighbor?" Jesus then proceeds to tell the story of the good Samaritan, one most of us know well. A Jewish man is beaten and left to die on the side of the road. Religious people—even a priest and a Levite—ignore him as they pass by. A Samaritan—someone of a different ethnicity and religion—stops to help, and ends up caring for the man as if he's his own biological brother.

Jesus's point could not be more clear. If we want to follow God and imitate Christ, we have no choice but to demonstrate our love to our neighbors. In my (Wayne's) book *Who Is My Neighbor?*, also published by Baker, I examine more than forty characteristics of the man who was beaten and left on the side of the road. I make it clear that our neighbors are not necessarily the ones who live close by, across the street, or on our cul-de-sac. My neighbors are those who are hurting, who've been beaten up, stripped, and left all alone. They are those who've been ignored by upstanding citizens and faithful churchgoers. They are those who have been made to feel as if their lives don't matter.

In Matthew 25, Jesus equates helping others with serving him: "I was hungry and you gave me something to eat, I was thirsty and you gave me something to drink, I was a stranger and you invited me in, I needed clothes and you clothed me, I was sick and you looked after me, I was in prison and you came to visit me" (vv. 35–36). Jesus then says, "Whatever you did for one of the least of these brothers and sisters of mine, you did for me" (v. 40).

Roadmap to Reconciliation

In addition to responding with compassion to those who have been mistreated, a truly Christian response to Black Lives Matter should be rooted in the pursuit of reconciliation. Reconciliation is, of course, a key theme in Christian theology, beginning with reconciling human beings with God through Christ. We are also called to reconcile with one another. Those who pursue reconciliation with people from a different cultural group or ethnicity almost always find that their lives—and their relationships—are enriched.

For most, reconciliation will not happen as part of a normal course of events. It has to be intentional. At Lawndale we recently completed a fourteen-week series titled "Real Relationships." This series challenged people to do the hard work of developing genuine relationships with people different from themselves. We used Brenda Salter McNeil's *Roadmap to Reconciliation*.* In this book, Salter McNeil cites two circles, each depicting a general approach to human behavior. The first is the circle of Preservation, which features isolation. The second is the circle of Transformation, which calls for reconciliation. The author observes that most people are just trying to survive life and thus find themselves in Preservation mode most if not all of the time. This leads to isolation, resulting in very few opportunities for relationships that take them outside their comfort zones.

Salter McNeil posits that moving from the Preservation circle to the Transformation circle often requires some kind of catalytic event. For many around the nation, this catalytic event has come in the form of one or more of the recent police shootings of African Americans—Trayvon Martin, Michael Brown, Freddie Gray, Alton Sterling, Philando Castile, and others. The catalytic event that hit both Chicago and the nation hard was the killing of seventeen-year-old Laquan McDonald in October 2014. He was shot by a Chicago police officer sixteen times in less than fifteen seconds. Most of the shots were fired after McDonald had fallen to the ground.

Police shootings and the prevailing culture of violence in our communities have spawned outrage, outrage to which the Black Lives Matter movement has given voice. Some have chosen to oppose it; some have chosen to ignore it. We believe it's time for Christians to support it and to view it as a pathway to reconciliation.

The overwhelming majority of those who have become victims of police shootings and our violent culture are people who have been marginalized. They are, by and large, voiceless—in need of an advocate. We need to respond to this opportunity, allowing Proverbs 31:8–9 to serve as our guide: "Speak up for those who

*Brenda Salter McNeil, *Roadmap to Reconciliation* (Downers Grove, IL: Inter-Varsity, 2016).

cannot speak for themselves, for the rights of all who are destitute. Speak up and judge fairly; defend the rights of the poor and needy."

We can think of no better way to proclaim to the world that all lives do indeed matter.

7

From Tears to Action

The topic for my sermon at Lawndale Community Church on April 1, 2012, was the kingdom of God. My text was the eighth chapter of Zechariah: "Once again men and women of ripe old age will sit in the streets of Jerusalem, each of them with cane in hand because of their age. The city streets will be filled with boys and girls playing there" (vv. 4–5).

It was the first of our two morning services. As I was unpacking this passage, I observed that in our urban communities these days we don't have boys and girls playing in the streets nor elderly sitting and watching them. The streets have become too dangerous, and our two most vulnerable demographic groups—the very old and the very young—no longer feel safe.

By April 1, the year 2012 had already witnessed ten murders in North Lawndale. One of them was Rekia Boyd, who, though unarmed, had been killed by an off-duty Chicago police officer. As I discussed the violence in our community, in an instant I became overwhelmed with grief and sadness. I began to weep profusely, uncontrollably. I couldn't stop. It turned into more than just weeping.

Tears began streaming down my face right in the middle of my sermon. I was barely able to finish.

After the service, Anne and I went to the high school Sunday school class, which we were coteaching. As we sat together, Anne patted me on my leg and asked, "Honey, are you okay?" Obviously what she and others had witnessed at the first service was not typical, not "normal" for me. I told her I was alright, but she apparently wasn't convinced, as she asked if I would be able to preach at the second service later that morning. I assured her I didn't have "cry here" in my notes and that I would be just fine.

At the second service, when I got to the same place in my sermon I again began talking about how our children can no longer play double Dutch or baseball in the streets, and the elderly can't sit and enjoy them because there is too much violence—too many drive-by shootings. Despite my assurances that I would be fine the second time around, I once again began to weep and then to cry uncontrollably. In fact, it was worse than the first service.

The very next day, the starting quarterback on one of the football teams I had coached at Farragut High School back in the '70s was shot eight times at point-blank range by a Chicago police officer. I went over to the scene where it happened. I sat in my car and began to cry as I mourned the death of Ricky Bradley. For the next six months, hardly a day went by that I didn't cry. Anne and I began to wonder if this ministry had become too much for me and for our family. Perhaps we needed to make a change.

Or perhaps what was happening to me was good. Perhaps it was necessary. Perhaps what hadn't been "normal" for me needed to become a sort of new normal. Maybe crying ought to be interpreted as a sign of truly understanding and entering the pain of others, a dynamic that can fuel compassion and lead to action on behalf of those who are having trouble believing that their lives matter.

Instead of ignoring or suppressing our pain and the pain of others, maybe we all need to cry more, not less. But we should also be careful not to allow our sadness and grief to keep us from taking action. Back in 2012, when I began finding it difficult to control my emotions, Anne suggested to me that perhaps God was calling us to do something to stop the violence in our community. She'd heard about training focused on promoting alternatives to violence, and so she gathered some of the leaders in the church, including Darryl Saffore, Darrin Brown, Randy Brown, Tiffany Price, Angelica Rainey, and Joe Atkins, to start brainstorming about what we might do to stop the violence.

This led to twenty-five people pursuing training in alternatives to violence. Ten of these twenty-five went on to become certified instructors. They now teach people how to resist the temptation to commit a violent act and to choose peaceful alternatives. At this writing, more than fifty people have completed the Lawndale Violence Alternative Training Program. This program makes use of role-playing situations that often lead to anger and then a violent act. Just acting out the various scenarios leads to learning new kinds of responses when angry. The class does a lot of brainstorming about options to violence and how to be angry without letting it lead to a violent action. Just learning how to stop for five seconds before acting greatly cuts down on the odds that an individual will commit a violent act. The training also involves a lot of personal interaction with each other and builds community among the participants.

This ministry, led by Anne, is one of several things the church has done over the last four years in pursuit of our goal of stopping the violence. We've also begun to talk more at Sunday morning services about the shootings and the people being murdered in our community. We use maps to show where people have been killed, making sure to note their names to honor their dignity as persons. Also for the past four years, every Wednesday we have called our church to fast. During the fast a group of fifteen to thirty people gather at the church at noon to pray together for half an hour. We get on our knees each week to express our love for our community and to beseech God to bring an end to the violence so that the streets might be safe again for the children to play and for the elderly to watch over them with canes in hand.

No one can say for sure what difference, if any, we have made so far. The Lawndale community continues to be plagued with violence. But we won't stop speaking up or taking action to end the violence. We will grieve every death but we will also go beyond tears. We won't stop doing everything we can do to make sure the world knows we believe that all lives matter.

8

Let Us Sow Love

Laws might change behavior but they cannot change hearts. A true revolution in our country—one that claims victory over violence and eliminates all exclusions to the proclamation that all lives matter—will come only as hearts are changed and as we recognize who our neighbors are and learn to truly love them as ourselves. As discussed in the previous chapter, we can hasten this process by making an effort to listen to others and to feel and enter into their pain.

A changed heart leads to positive action. But it's also true that taking action can lead to a changed heart. With this in mind, what follows are eleven suggestions—several of them interrelated—of things we can do to demonstrate the conviction that all lives matter.

1. Pray and Discuss the Prayer of St. Francis of Assisi on a Regular Basis

Lord, make me an instrument of your peace. Where there is hatred, let me sow love; where there is injury, pardon; where there is doubt, faith; where there is despair, hope; where there is darkness, light; where there is sadness, joy. O, Divine Master, grant that I may not so much seek to be consoled as to console; to be understood as to understand; to be loved as to love; for it is in giving that we receive; it is in pardoning that we are pardoned; it is in dying that we are born again to eternal life.

Since I was introduced to this prayer, I have personally prayed it often. In fact, I have memorized it, and the Holy Spirit often brings the prayer to my mind in difficult situations when I'm tempted with a revengeful or retaliatory spirit.

Pray this prayer and meditate on it once a day for at least a month. After that, return to it regularly. Consider praying it together with your family or small group. Make it a topic of discussion so that it becomes real—second nature—in your life.

2. Seek First to Understand, Then to Be Understood

This important concept from the above prayer is not just a spiritual concept but a practical one as well. In fact, Stephen Covey in his classic book *7 Habits of Highly Effective People* cites it as a fundamental principle. Focusing on others instead of ourselves demonstrates emotional intelligence and compassion.

What a difference it would make if we would all make a concerted effort to understand people who are different from us! Our friend Dr. Jawanza Kunjufu observes that this is a particularly important goal when developing relationships across racial lines. According to Kunjufu, we must first acknowledge that we have differences. Then we must strive to understand our differences. However, genuine reconciliation and healing take root only as we appreciate and celebrate our differences, as opposed to merely living with them.

3. Build and Cultivate Relationships across Ethnic Lines

It's often the case that the main contact church people have with different ethnic groups comes through a mission or service project. As helpful as these can be in terms of opening people's eyes to the realities others face, this is not what we are talking about here. In fact, it often happens that when white people come into troubled places for short periods of time they create more problems than they solve. For thorough treatments of this dynamic, consult Robert Lupton's *Toxic Charity* and Steve Corbett and Brian Fikkert's *When Helping Hurts: How to Alleviate Poverty without Hurting the Poor . . . and Yourself.*

We have in mind not putting Band-Aids on perceived problems but rather entering into genuine relationships with others. This requires escaping our cocoons and venturing outside of our comfort zones in order to do new and challenging things. For white folks, it entails reading books written by people of color and going to places and attending events organized and led by minority people. It means not just visiting churches that represent other cultures and ethnicities but fully participating in their worship.

Other possible steps include inviting people who are different to your Sunday school classes, small groups, and social activities. Don't allow the conversation to remain on the surface; pursue meaningful and significant dialogue. Perhaps even plan a discussion around a question or topic that is likely to bring out differing opinions and perspectives. Make sure everyone feels safe expressing their opinions, controversial though they may be.

4. Strive to Build Friendships with People Who Are Different

This is not just about race or ethnicity. It could be with people who are younger or older, or with someone with a different educational background or different interests in life. If you are a Republican, build a relationship with a Democrat. It's not about who is right and who is wrong but about looking at life from different perspectives. We can learn a lot—and grow a lot—from hanging out with those with whom we differ.

This also includes befriending people of other religions. Start having coffee or lunch with a Muslim or Jewish person. Or a Buddhist or an atheist. Remember that each of us bears the image of God and that no matter what our religious beliefs, our lives matter. Remember also that each interaction with people who are different exercises our capacity to understand and empathize with others.

5. Listen to the Music of Other Cultures

In case you were wondering: yes, this includes rap. Of course some rap is vulgar, promotes violence, and is demeaning to women. It would be wise to talk to others familiar with rap to suggest some music to listen to that would be informative and helpful. It might be outside your preferred musical tastes, but at the very least you can think about and reflect on the lyrics—what's being said, the messages being conveyed—and how they might affect your understanding of others and the struggles they are facing. Find a rap aficionado who can tutor you as to the meaning of certain words and phrases. You will receive an education! And you never know; the style and rhythm might just start to grow on you.

6. Move into a Diverse Community

If you transfer to a new place, instead of moving into a community just like the one you left, take a risk. Leave your comfort zone and find one that is integrated or perhaps one of a predominantly different ethnicity or culture. Talk to people who've made this kind of move. Hint: most will tell you they would do it all over again.

Dr. Greg Lee, a Korean American and assistant professor of theology at Wheaton College, along with his Korean American wife, Jeanette, moved into Lawndale and has commuted to Wheaton for the last four years. They now have two children and have developed into an important voice for race relations, poverty, and reconciliation. Greg's lectures at Wheaton are filled with stories of how God has used Lawndale in their lives to help them understand life from a different perspective. Greg has been coming to a weekly men's Bible study since he moved to Lawndale and has been very careful not to come as an expert but to remain a listener willing to learn from the men of Lawndale. The Lees have become a significant part of the Lawndale Community Church family and are deeply respected and loved.

7. Allow the Right Books and Movies to Inform and Inspire You

Don't underestimate how much the ideas expressed in books and movies can teach and inspire. Earlier we mentioned the teaching series based on Brenda Salter McNeil's book *Roadmap to Reconciliation*. She cites four steps on the road map: (1) Realization—understanding the new reality, (2) Identification—"Your people become my people," (3) Preparation—getting ready for lasting change, and (4) Activation—actively working for reconciliation. This brief paragraph suggests how much there is to be learned in this resource, one we highly recommend for individuals or groups. We invite you to use this book, too, as a focus for discussion in your home, office, Sunday School class, or other setting. Here is a list of books that we recommend as you continue your journey:

A Fellowship of Differents by Scot McKnight
America's Original Sin by Jim Wallis
Between the World and Me by Ta-Nehisi Coates
Beyond Charity by John M. Perkins
Brainwashed by Tom Burrell

Divided by Faith by Michael Emerson and Christian Smith

Dream with Me by John M. Perkins

Family Properties by Beryl Satter

Fist Stick Knife Gun by Geoffrey Canada

Jesus and the Disinherited by Howard Thurman

Just Mercy by Bryan Stevenson

Leadership Revolution by John M. Perkins and Wayne Gordon

Let Justice Roll Down by John M. Perkins

Making Neighborhoods Whole by Wayne Gordon and John M.
   Perkins

*Not without a Struggle: Leadership Development for African
   American Women in Ministry* by Vashti McKenzie

Race Matters by Cornel West

Real Hope in Chicago by Wayne Gordon

Red Brown Yellow Black White by LeRoy Barber

Redeeming Sex by Debra Hirsch

Roadmap to Reconciliation by Brenda Salter McNeil

Slavery by Another Name by Douglas A. Blackmon

The Irresistible Revolution by Shane Claiborne

The New Jim Crow by Michelle Alexander

The Next Evangelicalism by Soong-Chan Rah

The Promised Land by Nicholas Lemann

The Radical King edited by Cornel West

Toxic Charity by Bob Lupton

Where the Cross Meets the Street by Noel Castellanos

Who Is My Neighbor? by Wayne Gordon

With Justice for All by John M. Perkins

Have a movie night in your home where you feel safe to talk
about your feelings and where you will not be judged by your honest

comments. Maybe just with your spouse, older children, or possibly a couple of very close friends. We recommend the following movies:

Roots (the new 2016 series)
12 Years a Slave
Amistad
Amazing Grace (the story of William Wilberforce)
Crash
Guess Who's Coming to Dinner
Selma
42
The Great Debaters
The Birth of a Nation

After viewing any of these with a group, be sure to discuss your thoughts and feelings—and also how you might think and live differently from now on. Keep in mind that some of the above films are rated R and include violent scenes and bad language. They are not all appropriate for children. A few children's movie possibilities are:

The Long Walk Home
McFarland
Pride
Woodlawn
Ruby Bridges

8. Participate in a Discussion Group

A discussion group constitutes the perfect venue for reflecting on the issues of the day and the questions facing our churches and communities. John and I have both had wonderful opportunities to interact with people who desire to talk deeply about what's going on in our world today. When he is home in Jackson, Mississippi, John attends a discussion group on Friday mornings at which hard topics regularly show up front and center. The group includes several young people from Jackson State University.

The size or makeup of a group is unimportant. I have the great privilege of having breakfast every Saturday morning (when we are all in town) with a very small group—me and my two sons, Andrew and Austin, at Manny's, a local Jewish delicatessen. We have extremely deep dialogue about the world's hot topics, and I've learned to value their younger perspectives. We often talk for two to three hours. Such a blessing and learning time.

9. Support Restorative Justice Policies and Efforts

Restorative justice is starting to become an alternative to "lock them up." Search out where there is talk and discussion of this in your communities. Restorative justice is essentially a community-led response to crime and conflict. It emphasizes the ways in which crime harms relationships in the context of community, attempting to bring together all affected parties in an effort to arrive at resolution. Restorative justice represents an alternative to the current punitive system of justice. Instead of viewing crimes as being committed against the state, it focuses on the harm that has been done to the community and to individuals within it.

The current system emphasizes doling out punishment that is appropriate for the crime. Often the punishment is extreme to the individual and costly to the state. It can easily cause further damage to a community that has already been harmed and it relies almost exclusively on incarceration and permanent felony stigmatization as the two main responses to crime. This approach has failed us, not only causing many to believe that their lives do not matter but also costing taxpayers an exorbitant amount of money and devastating primarily black communities.

Restorative justice focuses on healing communities, not on punishment. This emphasis on healing brings greater accountability and support for the offender as well as restoration of the victim and affected community members. Arguably, there is not less accountability in restorative justice but significantly more. Our legal center, Lawndale Christian Legal Center, is helping to lead restorative justice initiatives in Chicago. Get involved in restorative justice in your community and learn the benefits of this philosophy of justice.

10. Consider Organizing or Joining a Peaceful Protest

It's possible to reach a point at which staging some kind of visible public protest is almost the only way voices can be heard and injustice can be exposed. Anne and I, along with many others from Lawndale Community Church, have arrived at this point on more than one occasion. Engaging in a protest can be both risky and messy. It can be risky because although the call is for peace, the history of protests has shown that it's possible for frustration in one quarter or another to bubble over into violence. And it can be messy in that we can find ourselves aligned with people whose agendas and ideas we don't always completely share.

Earlier I discussed the killing of Laquan McDonald, a Lawndale resident who was shot sixteen times by a Chicago police officer. Video of this shooting was held for over a year before being released on November 24, 2015. The world was horrified. Any doubt about what had actually happened was erased by the footage.

Twenty other pastors and I stood with Chicago Mayor Rahm Emanuel and the police superintendent, hoping and praying both for peace and for justice, when the video was made public. Thousands of people felt like they had to do something to show their disapproval and dismay. Many from our church went down to Michigan Avenue on Black Friday, the biggest shopping day of the year. Anne and I were among the more than five thousand people who blocked traffic as part of an orderly march of protest. Jesse Jackson and Congressman Danny Davis also participated.

Three people were arrested that day for blocking traffic. Two of them—Josiah Daniels and Ben Swihart, both Perkins scholars at Northern Seminary where John and I team-teach urban ministry— were from our ministry. In their blog they stated,

> This Black Friday in Chicago, protesters followed Jesus' example by making a spectacle of the powers and principalities by nonviolently preventing people from entering the "temples" of the Magnificent Mile shopping district. The response to that act demonstrated how capitalism shapes people's desires so much that outrage over the murders of Rekia Boyd and Laquan McDonald become afterthoughts in comparison to the itch for a good bargain.*

11. Work with the Police and Leaders of Your City or Community

Along with African American pastors Johnny Miller and James Meeks, I have been meeting with the mayor and leaders in the Chicago police department to try to build better relationships between police and the communities they serve. We are trying to determine what can be done to bridge the communication gap—to help our community and the police understand one another so we can unite against the violence. No city wants to be known for its murder statistics.

Several things have emerged from these meetings. Pastors have had district commanders come to their churches on Sunday morning to share a few words from their perspective and so the people of local churches can pray for them. We are working hard in our respective districts to build deeper relationships.

*Ben Swihart and Josiah Daniels, "16 Shots and the Importance of Disruption," *Smoldering Hope*, November 30, 2015, https://smolderinghope.com/2015/11/.

One morning, during the Sunday school hour at Lawndale Community Church, we formed a panel consisting of our district commander, Frank Valadez; a deputy chief from police headquarters, Eric Washington; and a beat police officer who serves the Lawndale community, Kamryn Schwarz. Our church people were free to ask any question or bring up any issue with the police, and we were all able to listen to one another and share concerns as part of our search for common ground and a unified strategy. It was a rewarding time and experience of bringing our community and police closer together. We laid hands on the officers and prayed for them. As a sign of our support for police, after the killings of officers in Dallas, several of the youth ministries of our neighborhood churches went to the district police headquarters to deliver snacks and water and to pray for them.

Pastors Miller and Meeks and I have been on "ride alongs" with our district commanders in order to better understand the streets and the role of those who police them. I went on my ride along late on a Friday night in August and found it to be quite eye-opening. It helped me to better understand what our police officers do and what they are up against. I have a fond memory from that night. As we drove past a crowd of people at three a.m., I thought I recognized a few young people from our church. I asked the officer to drive past that spot again. As we pulled up in front of these people, they approached the car. Some were a bit startled to see me as I rolled down my window in the passenger seat, and said, "Hey, Coach, we didn't expect to see you here."

I called the ones I knew by name and asked them what in the world they were doing. Turns out they were just standing around and talking, enjoying one another's company. Not every interaction between police and black youth is a bad encounter, even on a Chicago street corner at three in the morning.

I have committed to pray for all the police officers who attend Lawndale Community Church. I daily pray that God will keep them safe and give them wisdom. In the summer of 2016, two African American police officers from our church—Yolanda and Duane—volunteered at our summer program every week. They came in uniform and encouraged our kids to get to know them.

It's sad and disheartening to hear that some urban youth believe they can't trust police. Sadder still to think that some have learned this lesson from experience. We need to work to change this, and it begins by applying the advice offered earlier in this chapter—we need to build relationships with others in an effort to understand them. As the old song puts it, "The more we get together, the happier we'll be."

Please do what you can to proclaim to the world that all lives matter. Some may march in protest. Some may pray. Some may write letters. Some may blog. Some may write poetry and songs. It might be that some can only weep. But we all need to do something. And as we do, we obey Christ's command to love God with every fiber of our beings and to love our neighbors as ourselves. Let's treat all people as if their lives do matter.

9

Holding On to Hope

We could probably fill an entire book with stories of people who have had so many confrontations with police—or who have been told so many times and in so many different ways that their lives don't matter—that they have begun to lose hope.

At Lawndale we often discuss what our biggest problem might be. Is it a lack of jobs? Is it poor schools? Crime and violence? Fatherless children? We have all of the above and more. But if you ask me, our biggest problem is that so many people living here have lost hope. In fact, one could argue that the whole Black Lives Matter movement is rooted in a desperate attempt to hold on to hope by rejecting the message that some lives don't matter.

When people are treated as if their lives don't matter, they inevitably get discouraged and begin to lose hope. It can be very difficult not to act out. Dr. Jawanza Kunjufu has observed that only those who have lost hope and who no longer love themselves will shoot somebody who looks like them.

Virtually every day we see people in our community who have given up. Life for them has become a fight for survival. They just want to crawl into a corner. They've been told so many times that no one loves them that they no longer love themselves. They've stopped living; they've lost hope. It's little wonder that so many have turned to drugs and to other self-destructive behaviors.

At Lawndale we have noticed a relationship between hope and work. In fact, the number one question men ask is, "Can you get me a job?" Despite what some may think, most people want to work. Through work, they gain a sense of self-worth and dignity. Having a job suggests they are making a difference. People take pride in providing for their families and contributing to society. In a word, a job provides hope. Conversely, the unemployed have a sense of hopelessness. We see it in men's lives virtually every day.

In an effort to encourage people not to give up, over twenty years ago at Lawndale we established Hope House. Hope House is a recovery home for men. Some have been strung out on drugs, some are returning to the community from prison, some have been living on the streets, and some are dealing with other challenges and issues. A favorite verse of people who come through Hope House is Jeremiah 29:11, where God says, "I know the plans I have for you . . . plans to prosper you and not to harm you, plans to give you hope and a future." This verse has, over the years, offered hope to many people who have been pushed in many different ways to the margins of our world. We help them to find both hope and a new life in Jesus Christ.

Wardell Tate remembers the day when he was sixteen years old and his mother, who was crossing the street, was hit by a car. She was dragged for almost a block before being dropped right near the front of their house, where Wardell was standing. The driver kept going; Wardell's mom died. He went into the house and stayed in his bedroom for five days. He'd received the message that his mother's life didn't matter. He felt his life didn't matter either. Hopelessness set in, and he turned to a life of gangs and drugs for the next twenty years before finally coming through Hope House, where Christ gave him a new life, one filled with hope.

There was a time when Pastor Joe Atkins, mentioned at times throughout this book, had given up on life. One night he took a razor blade and slit his wrists, hoping to die. He was desperate, discouraged, depressed, and despondent. He'd lost hope. But thanks be to the Lord, he didn't die. And on that night he determined that if he wasn't able to die, he wanted to get right. Today, not only is he our associate pastor but also the leader of Hope House.

We have seen too many lives turned around to ever give up. We know from experience that hope can give way to change.

As you live in ways that proclaim that all lives matter, you will more than likely lose some arguments. You will lose elections and battles over public policy. You might even lose some of your friends as a result of standing up for what you believe and for doing what you know is right. But whatever else you lose, I encourage you to never lose hope. Always live believing that what is good and right and true and just will, in God's time, emerge victorious.

ALL LIVES DO MATTER!

Afterword

I was raised in New Jersey, and by age seven I was already an avid Brooklyn Dodgers fan. I know I was actively rooting for "da Bums" by then because Jackie Robinson played his first game for the Dodgers at second base when I was that age, and I have vivid memories of what all of that meant at the time. Some of my relatives, also Dodgers fans, were not all that happy about the first "colored guy" to don a major league uniform. I did not get into arguments with them about it, but I silently cheered Jackie on. I will never forget the thrill, listening to the broadcast of the game on the radio (we did not have television in our home yet), when during his rookie season he stole home plate during a game with the Pirates.

To have taken his plight seriously as a child was to sense something about the realities of racial prejudice. That awareness was reinforced a few years later, on a family visit to Florida, where in a public place I deliberately went to drink water from the "colored" drinking fountain. A policeman who saw me approach the fountain rushed over, yanked me away, and reprimanded me sternly.

Those events nurtured real racial sympathies in my heart—but they were still only isolated ones in my life. The events did not lead me to think about patterns or structures.

My first real awareness of issues regarding the systemic character of American racism came in my late teens at a church gathering. I had gone with my dad to observe a meeting of our denomination's annual synod, and on that occasion the delegates were discussing a motion to call for open housing—a rather new topic for many of us white folks in the late 1950s. There was much opposition expressed to the idea of "legislating morality." Several speakers emphasized the need to concentrate solely on promoting more love between the races. "Only changed hearts will change society" was a refrain repeated several times.

There was one African American delegate to that synod, an elder from a West Coast congregation. Toward the end of the discussion he rose to speak. He and his wife, he said, had driven across the country for him to attend that denominational gathering. For one whole day on their journey, he reported, they had not been able to buy a meal, because no restaurant would serve them. In one instance, he said, there were a dozen empty tables available but a waitress told them there was no place for them to be seated. Then he uttered a couple of sentences that made a deep impression on me: "It would be wonderful if that waitress *loved* us. But right then we were not asking for love—we wanted *cheeseburgers!*"

Having heard his speech, it did not surprise me when, not long after that, cheeseburgers—access to lunch counters—figured significantly into the early organized protests against segregation. Subsequently, I was greatly motivated to get engaged in the struggle for civil rights by Dr. King's eloquent Lincoln Memorial address. But in many ways his inspiring words were for me an elaboration on that black elder's stirring plea for the right to buy a cheeseburger on a cross-country journey.

Much has happened in the quest for racial equality since those days in my youth. The waitress in that western state would be in legal trouble today if she blatantly refused to serve black patrons.

Along with many other things, the right of black families to purchase cheeseburgers has been secured. But the journey is far from over.

I am convinced that the important issues raised by the Black Lives Matter movement is a challenge for us as Christians to take a new look at the old "changed hearts" refrain. Legislation has been absolutely necessary in the struggle. Absolutely. But in our complex democratic system, laws can be not only inconsistently applied but also revised and revoked. The legislative gains in the cause of justice need a deeper reinforcement if the true goals of making these laws are to be sustained.

While racism is indeed a violation of the demands of justice, it is more than that. It is, for one thing, a theological heresy. But, more importantly for the challenges that presently face us, it is also a serious—a devastatingly serious—spiritual defect. It is one thing to say that the right to buy cheeseburgers matters, as well as the right to enroll one's children in quality schools and the right to register to vote. But it goes much deeper to say—and to really *mean* it—that black *lives* matter.

We need to be preaching this. Black lives matter because every black person is a special creation, fashioned in the image of God the Father of Jesus Christ. They matter because the Lord God takes delight in human flourishing. They matter because God cares about families and neighborhoods and elections and skillful plays at second base.

The theology that recognizes and emphasizes all of that, however, needs to be sustained by a deep spirituality of love for our neighbors. Jesus paid the debt for the sin of racism. And he shed his blood to incorporate us into a community from many races and tribes and peoples and nations—into a new kind of "kingdom and priests to serve our God" (Rev. 5:10). We are not just talking about politics and theology—we are talking about the fundamental character of Christian *identity*.

Yes, it is certainly true that *all* lives matter to God. But there are times when we need to focus on specific lives because those lives have for too long been denied the right to flourish. And this focus must be generated out of hearts that have been shaped by desires that flow from the very heart of God.

I am grateful to Wayne and John for the gift they have made available to us by writing this wonderful book. They speak eloquently about the cause of justice but they also probe more deeply, calling us to share the Savior's grief over lives that have for too long known pain, suffering, and neglect. To receive the profound message of this book into the deep places of our own being is to nurture the genuine hope that changed hearts can indeed change society!

Richard J. Mouw
President Emeritus, Fuller Theological Seminary

Acknowledgments

We are so thankful for the opportunity to write this book. Many people have influenced us and helped us in our writing, most significantly our wives, Anne and Vera Mae. Also our children have helped us to see the world with younger eyes and fresh new perspectives: Angela, Andrew (Stacy), and Austin Gordon; Spencer, deceased (Nancy), Joanie (Ron), Phillip (Eva), Derek, Deborah, Wayne, Priscilla, and Elizabeth Perkins. Also our thirteen Perkins and two Gordon grandchildren.

We appreciate Dwight Baker for his willingness to help us go forward with our ideas in a timely manner with passion and encouragement. Thanks to Brian Thomasson for providing direction and editing and walking us through this process. Of course, we also wish to thank all of the Baker Publishing family, including David Baker, Abby Van Wormer, Erin Smith, Erin Bartels, Chad Allen, and Lindsey Spoolstra.

Special thanks to Randy Frame for helping us position our words and thoughts in a readable manner. Randy has such a wonderful ability to make our ideas and thoughts flow with ease and clarity. Thank you, friend.

We also are appreciative of Gordon Murphy for helping with research for this book, and to Willette Grant for her willingness and hard work in typing and retyping our manuscript. Also thanks to Linda Burk, who worked to help flesh out chapter 2.

Of course we are so thankful for our friends in Chicago, our church families in Lawndale and Jackson, and the CCDA family. We love you all.

Wayne Gordon is cofounder of the Christian Community Development Association and lead pastor of Lawndale Community Church in inner-city Chicago, where he has ministered for over forty years. He and Lawndale Community Church have founded Lawndale Christian Health Center, Lawndale Christian Development Corporation, Lawndale Christian Legal Center, and Hope House. He is the author of several books, including *Real Hope in Chicago* and *Who Is My Neighbor?* He and his wife, Anne, have three adult children.

John M. Perkins is cofounder of the Christian Community Development Association and president emeritus of the John M. Perkins foundation for Reconciliation and Development in Jackson, Mississippi. He has founded Christian Community Development ministries in Mendenhall, Mississippi; Pasadena, California; and Jackson, Mississippi. He is the author of many books, including *Beyond Charity* and *Let Justice Roll Down*, named by *Christianity Today* as one of the top fifty books that have shaped evangelicals. He and his wife, Vera Mae, live in Jackson.